Carol Deacon's Little Book of

Easy Cake Charac

Carol Deacon CAKES

www.caroldeaconcakes.com

Fondant wishes!

Carol Deacon

Introduction

As I am constantly asked about how to make little icing animals and people, it seemed logical to put together a book that deals with just this. I have crammed in as much information and as many ideas as I could and hope it will inspire you to have a go.

As this book concentrates solely on modelling and creating little characters, there is no recipe for baking the cake itself as this would have taken up valuable space. However you can find my cake recipes in any of my other books or on the website www.caroldeaconcakes.com I hope you enjoy using this book and do send me pictures of your cakes.

Fondant wishes

Carol Deacon

Contents

Sugarpaste

Sugarpaste is basically an edible modelling paste. So, if you have ever made anything out of modelling clay then you already possess the skills needed to use sugarpaste.

Sugarpaste is called by many different names around the world including fondant, rolled fondant, ready to roll icing and even plastic icing because of its stretchy and malleable properties. It is designed for covering cakes and making small models. It is not the same as flowerpaste or petal paste. As cake decorating has grown in popularity, so has the availability of cake decorating materials and sugarpaste is now available from most supermarkets as well as cake decorating outlets. There are many brands available and even the supermarket own brands are usually very good. The best thing about working with sugarpaste though is that anyone can use it – from the very young to the young at heart!

Sugarpaste Recipe

If you prefer to make your own paste, the recipe is pretty straightforward but it is a bit of a sticky process and is easiest made using a food mixer. This recipe should produce enough sugarpaste to cover a 18cm (7in) round cake.

Ingredients

500g (1lb 2oz) icing sugar
1 egg white or equivalent dried egg white (meringue powder) reconstituted
30 ml (2 tablespoons) liquid glucose

1 Sieve the sugar into a large bowl and make a well in the centre.

2 Tip the egg white and glucose into the well and stir it in. If you're doing this by hand, use a knife and hold it almost vertical to bind the ingredients together.

3 Once mixed, use your hands or the bread kneading attachment on your mixer to knead the fondant. Knead the dough until it becomes silky and smooth.

4 Double wrap the fondant in two plastic food bags to prevent it from drying out. It can be used immediately. It does not have to be refrigerated but should be used within a week.

Covering a cake

Although this is a book about making decorations for your cakes, I thought it might be worth including a few brief instructions about covering a cake with sugarpaste just in case you've never tackled that before. There are recipes for both cakes and buttercream on the website www.caroldeaconcakes.com

1 Split and fill your sponge cake with buttercream then reassemble the cake. Place it onto your cake board and coat the outside of the cake with buttercream. Place a little plastic wrap over the coated cake to keep the buttercream soft while you prepare the sugarpaste.

2 Dust your work surface with a little icing sugar and knead your sugarpaste until it is soft and pliable. You will need about 800g (1lb 12oz) to cover a 20cm (8in) round cake. Roll out the sugarpaste to about 5mm (1/2in) thick.

3 Remove the plastic wrap off the cake and lift and place the sugarpaste over the top of the cake. You an either use a rolling pin to lift it or slide your hands palms uppermost under the icing and lift it keeping your palms flat. If it's sticking to your work surface, slide a palette knife underneath the icing to release it.

4 Once over the cake, smooth the top of the cake first with the flat of your hands. This is to try to prevent air from getting trapped beneath and forming air bubbles. Then gently push, press and coax the sugarpaste around the sides of the cake.

5 If you have a cake smoother, run it over the top and sides. These innocuous looking bits of flat plastic with handles are how you achieve a professional flat finish. They are used like an iron to smooth out any lumps, dents or fingerprints.

6 Using a small sharp knife, trim away the excess icing from around the base of the cake.

Air Bubbles

Also worth mentioning is the dreaded air bubble that sometimes occurs when air gets trapped beneath the sugarpaste as for some reason they never happen at the back of a cake! Prick the bulge with a clean dressmaker's needle or cocktail stick held at an angle and carefully press the air out.

Storing Your Covered Cake

Once covered, the sponge beneath the sugarpaste is effectively sealed and airtight so will remain edible for 4-5 days so you can usually prepare your cake a few days in advance of the party.

Your precious cake is then best stored in a cardboard cake box as airtight plastic boxes will make the sugarpaste "sweat". It does not need to be kept in a fridge and sugarpasted cakes cannot be frozen. A box will also protect it from dust and flies.

Colouring Sugarpaste

Shop bought sugarpaste is available in many colours or you can create your own with food colour. To do this it is best to use paste or gel colours as these are thicker than traditional liquid colours. As they're thicker, they shouldn't affect the consistency of the icing when you knead them in. Use a fresh cocktail stick to apply the colour then knead it in.

As you begin to knead, a marbled effect will begin to appear in the sugarpaste. This can be useful if you're trying to achieve a water or woodgrain effect. If you want a flat matt colour, continue kneading until the sugarpaste becomes a solid block of colour.

If the result is darker than you'd like, knead some white sugarpaste back in to lighten it. If it's too light, add more colour and continue kneading. Once you have achieved your desired shade, double wrap in small plastic food bags and store in an airtight plastic box until required.

As well as colouring sugarpaste with food pastes, you can also knead two lumps of sugarpaste together to make a different colour. For example, if you knead black and white together it will turn grey. Mix a tiny bit of red into yellow and you'll create orange.

Dark Colours

Because of the amount of food colour they require and the muscles involved in kneading, it's worth considering buying ready coloured deep, dark colours such as black or red. It is also worth buying ready coloured sugarpaste if you have to cover a very large cake as you can be confident the colour will be consistent throughout.

Flesh Tones

You can buy flesh coloured sugarpaste in various tones or you can colour your own using food pastes or by kneading different combinations of coloured sugarpaste together.

To create a pink flesh colour, use a food paste in a shade called "Paprika" or "chestnut". Alternatively knead a little pink, yellow and white sugarpaste together.

For darker skin tones, use brown food colour paste or knead a little green, red and black sugarpaste together.

For a golden colour, use a shade of colour paste called "Autumn leaf" or knead red, yellow and a little black sugarpaste together.

Using Sugarpaste

Sugarpaste is very easy to use but there are a few points you should be aware of.

Keep it wrapped

Always keep unused sugarpaste tightly wrapped to stop it drying out. Store your wrapped sugarpaste in an airtight plastic box. It does not need to be kept in a fridge.

Once it's got to the crusty stage it becomes unusable and your only option is to slice the dried section off and discard it.

Icing Sugar

Keep a little bowl of icing sugar nearby. Use this to dust your work surface when rolling out sugarpaste and to keep your fingers from getting too sticky. Some people use a little white vegetable fat to roll their sugarpaste out on. If you prefer to use fat then be very sparing. There is no definitive right or wrong way – use whatever works for you.

Sticking Sugarpaste

You can just use plain water and a soft paintbrush to stick your models together but make sure you just use light dabs of water or your models will start dissolving. Alternatively you can use sugar glue. You buy this or make your own by dissolving a lump of sugarpaste in a small glass of water.

Make up the individual pieces of your model and stick them together as you go. The "exploded" photos in this book are intended as a guide only. If you make all the components first then try and stick them together, you'll find the bits you made at the beginning will have started to dry out and will probably crack.

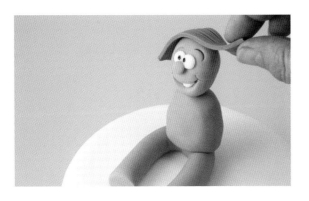

Additives

Apart from colour you shouldn't need to add anything else to your sugarpaste for any of the characters in this book. But if you prefer using a firmer and slightly stronger paste, you can knead in a little CMC or Gum Tragacanth (both available from cake decorating outlets). Knead about 1 teaspoon for every 250g (8oz) of sugarpaste. The CMC should start to thicken the sugarpaste immediately and can be used straight away. With the Gum Tragacanth, you should wait 24 hours before using it.

Spaghetti

To keep your models upright it's very tempting to poke a cocktail stick down the middle to stop them leaning. It is best to avoid this if possible just in case some unsuspecting soul tries to bite the head off one of your little people. Instead use a small section of uncooked spaghetti. Poke it through the body and into the cake beneath. Usually you would leave about 2.5cm (1in) protruding on which to slot the head.

Always let the recipient know about any internal supports.

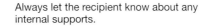

Cleaning

If you have a few dusty icing sugar marks on your decorations, simply brush them away with a soft, damp paintbrush. The sugarpaste surface will look shiny for a while as it dries but will eventually revert back to its original matt finish.

Warming up

If your sugarpaste is very cold you can soften it in the microwave. Just give it a short blast for about 10 seconds or so. Too long and it will melt and burn. This will not work on sugarpaste that has dried out. Once it's dried and crusty that's it.

Making Little People

Making a little person to put on your cake can seem a bit daunting especially if you've never attempted to make one before. However if you pull a character apart you will see that the individual components are actually very simple shapes. Ball, carrot, and sausage shapes are by far the most common shapes and these are very easy to create. Over the next few pages you can see how to create simple basic people. But remember these are just guidelines. Feel free to personalise your characters however you wish with different hairstyles, skin tones and outfits.

Man

You will need

30g (1oz) blue sugarpaste
40g (1 1/2oz) light brown sugarpaste
20g (2/3 oz) flesh coloured sugarpaste
Tiny bit of white sugarpaste
5g (1/8 oz) dark brown sugarpaste
5g (1/8 oz) black sugarpaste
1 strand raw uncooked spaghetti
Black food colour paste
Water for sticking
Icing sugar

Equipment

Paintbrush
Small rolling pin
Small sharp knife
Piping nozzle
Drinking straw
Cocktail stick

1 Begin with the legs. Roll about 30g (1oz) blue sugarpaste into a string about 18cm (7 in) long. Slice off the rounded ends and bend the legs into a horse shoe shape. Stick the legs onto the cake.

2 Mould about 30g (1 oz) brown sugarpaste into a cone for the body and stick on top of the legs. Poke a bit of spaghetti through the body to add support. Leave about 2.5cm (1in) protruding.

3 Roll about 15g (1/2oz) flesh coloured sugarpaste into a thick oval for the head. Press a piping nozzle into the lower part of the face and pull it downwards a little to create a curved smile.

4 Stick two tiny white balls onto the face for his eyes. If you want to add teeth, drop a tiny sliver of white into the mouth.

5 To create his cheeks and eyebrows, use the edge of a drinking straw to press tiny curves at the edges of the mouth and above the eyes.

6 Add a tiny flesh ball for his nose and put two black dots on the eyes with a cocktail stick dipped in a little black food colour paste.

7 To make the hair, roll out the dark brown sugarpaste and press lines into it. Cut out a rectangle and lay and stick over the head. Press a line onto the hair with the back of a knife to create his centre parting.

8 Make two tiny flesh coloured balls for the ears and stick one either side of the head. Poke the end of a paintbrush into each ear to create a little hollow.

9 Roll the remaining light brown sugarpaste into a thin string for the arms. Cut it in two and stick an arm either side of the body.

10 Roll the leftover flesh coloured paste into two small disks for the hands and stick one on the end of each arm.

Making Little People

Woman

Placing something such as a handbag onto a character's lap can not only be used to hide any problems that might have occurred but will also provide additional support for your model.

You will need

75g (2 1/2oz) blue sugarpaste
40g (1 1/2oz) flesh coloured sugarpaste
30g (1oz) brown sugarpaste
Tiny bit of white sugarpaste
Black and red food colour pastes
1 strand raw uncooked spaghetti
Water for sticking models
Icing sugar

Equipment

Paintbrushes fine & medium
Small sharp knife
Small rolling pin

1 Mould 60g (2oz) blue sugarpaste into a cone shape for the body then bend it in the middle so that it can sit upright on the cake.

2 Make a little flesh coloured disk for the neck and stick on top of the body. Poke a section of raw spaghetti into the body for support.

3 Roll about 15g (1/2oz) flesh coloured sugarpaste into a ball for the head. Add two tiny white disks for eyes and make three tiny cuts either side of each eye for the eyelashes.

4 Add a tiny flesh ball for the nose. Paint black food colour dots on the eyes and red food colour lips. This is not as hard as it might sound. Paint a red "M" shape on the top and a curved line beneath. Stick the head onto the body.

5 Roll out about 15g (1/2oz) brown sugarpaste for the hair. Press lines down the length with the back of a knife and cut out a long rectangle. Lay the rectangle over the head and press a parting into the hair with the back of a knife.

6 Cut out a little brown almond shape for the fringe and stick onto the hair.

7 Mould 10g brown sugarpaste into a thick semi-circle for the handbag and press a criss-cross pattern into one side with the back of your knife. Make a tiny brown handle. Stick the handbag in place on her lap.

8 To create the arms, roll 10g (1/3oz) blue sugarpaste into a string. Cut it in half and bend each arm at the elbow and stick onto the body. Add two tiny flesh disks for hands.

9 To make the legs, roll 10g (1/3oz) flesh coloured sugarpaste into a string about 10cm (4in) long. Cut it in half and gently squeeze the two rounded ends into points.

10 Make two small, thick blue triangles. Using the end of a paintbrush press a hollow into either shoe. Slot the leg into the shoe. Repeat on the other leg then stick the legs into place.

Making Little People

Teenage Boy

Know anyone this reminds you of ?
I do !!

You will need

25g (1oz) black sugarpaste
25g (1oz) blue sugarpaste
20g (2/3oz) flesh coloured sugarpaste
Tiny bit of white sugarpaste
15g (1/2oz) brown sugarpaste
Water for sticking
Icing sugar

Equipment

Paintbrush
Small rolling pin
Small sharp knife

1 Make a tiny flat black sugarpaste rectangle for the phone. Place this to one side and roll the rest of the black sugarpaste into a thin string about 23cm (9in) long for the legs. Bend the legs in half and arrange and stick in position on the cake.

2 Mould 15g (1/2oz) blue sugarpaste into a carrot shape for the body and stick next to the legs.

3 Roll 5g (1/8 oz) blue sugarpaste into a string about 9cm (4in) long. Bend in half and stick on the cake next to the top of the body.

4 Make a 15g (1/2oz) flesh coloured oval for the head and stick on top of both the arm and the top of the body. Press a sloping line for the mouth with the back of your knife.

5 Stick a tiny flesh coloured ball on the face for the nose and another on the side of the head for an ear.

6 Stick the phone on the cake next to the body. Roll a tiny bit of white into a thin string and drape and stick from the phone to the boy's ear. Stick a tiny ball of white on the boy's ear for his earplug.

7 Make a small flesh coloured oval for his hand and stick on top of the phone. Roll the rest of the blue into the second arm and stick into place across the body.

8 Roll out a little brown sugarpaste and cut out a semi-circle for the hair. Cut it into a fringe then lay and stick over the head.

9 Divide the remaining brown sugarpaste in half and roll into two ovals for the feet. Stick the feet at the end of the legs.

Making Little People

Teenage Girl

A phone and a big pouty mouth. Two important embellishments most teenage girls would never be seen without!

You will need

40g (1 1/2oz) black sugarpaste
40g (1 1/2oz) white sugarpaste
20g (2/3oz) flesh coloured sugarpaste
Tiny bit of yellow sugarpaste
30g (1oz) brown sugarpaste
1 strand raw uncooked spaghetti
Black and red food colour pastes
Water for sticking
Icing sugar

Equipment

Paintbrushes (fine & medium)
Bone tool (optional)
Small sharp knife
Small rolling pin

1 Roll 30g (1oz) black sugarpaste into a string about 20cm (8in) long for the girl's legs. Bend it in half and stick onto the cake.

2 Make a thick 10g (1/3oz) black sugarpaste oval and stick this onto the top of her legs. This is to give her body a little extra height.

3 Make a 20g (2/3oz) white cone for her jumper and stick upright on top of the black. Insert a little spaghetti for support if you wish and press a few spots onto the jumper with the end of a paintbrush.

4 To make the head, roll 15g (1/2oz) flesh coloured sugarpaste into a ball. Make two oval hollows for the eyes with a bone tool or the end of a paintbrush. Paint half the inside of each eye socket with black food colour and paint three eyelashes at the edge of each eye.

5 Add a nose and paint red food colour lips. Stick the head in place on the body.

6 To make the arms, roll 10g (1/3oz) white sugarpaste into a string and cut in half. Stick the arms in place.

7 Make two little flesh disk shapes for the hands and a tiny yellow rectangle for the phone. Stick the phone between the hands on her lap.

8 To make the hair, thinly roll out 30g (1oz) brown sugarpaste. Press lines into it with the back of your knife then cut out a long tombstone shape. Stick this at the back of her head.

9 Cut out two shorter rectangles and stick one either side of the head.

10 To make her trainers, divide 10g (1/3oz) white sugarpaste in half and make two small "L" shapes. Press three lines into the soles with the back of your knife.

Making Little People

Boy

This little character's T-shirt has sleeves. Although this is simply a matter of slicing a sugarpaste circle in half, it's a technique that you may find useful when dressing other little characters.

You will need

30g (1oz) brown sugarpaste
15g (1/2oz) white sugarpaste
5g (1/8oz) blue sugarpaste
30g (1oz) flesh coloured sugarpaste
5g (1/8oz) black sugarpaste
1 strand spaghetti
Black and red food colour
Water for sticking models
Icing sugar

Equipment

Paintbrush
Small sharp knife
Small rolling pin

1 Begin with his legs. Pull off a tiny bit of brown and put to one side to create the fringe later. Roll the rest into a sausage about 10cm (4in) long. Bend the legs into a horseshoe shape.

2 Make a 10g (1/3oz) white cone shape for the torso and stick on top of the legs. Add a section of spaghetti for support if you wish.

3 Make a little blue ball and stick onto his lap.

4 To make the arms, roll 5g (1/8oz) flesh coloured sugarpaste into a small string and cut in half. Stick one either side of the body with the hands on the ball.

5 To make the sleeves, cut a small white sugarpaste disk in half and stick one half over the top of each arm.

6 Make a 15g (1/2oz) flesh oval shape for the head. Add two white ovals for the eyes. Poke a paintbrush into the lower part of the face and pull downwards slightly to create the mouth.

7 Add a two tiny flesh ball shapes for the ears and one for the nose. Poke the end of a paintbrush into each ear to create a little hollow.

8 Paint two black dots on the eyes and dab a little watered down red food colour on the cheeks.

9 Cut out a small brown rectangle for the hair and cut a fringe along one edge. Stick the hair onto the head.

10 Divide the black sugarpaste in half and roll into two ovals for the shoes and stick one on the end of each leg.

Baby

As every parent knows, time simply disappears once a baby's on the scene so remember you can make your cake characters well in advance. Store them in a cardboard cake box somewhere cool (not the fridge) until they're needed.

You will need

60g (2oz) flesh coloured sugarpaste
5g (1/8oz) white sugarpaste
Tiny bit of brown sugarpaste
Black and red food colour
Water for sticking
Icing sugar

Equipment

Paintbrush
Small sharp knife
Small rolling pin
Drinking straw

1 To make the arms, roll 10g (1/3oz) flesh coloured sugarpaste into a thin string about 10cm (4in) long. Bend it into a sausage shape with the two ends meeting in the middle.

2 Make the body by rolling 15g (1/2oz) flesh coloured sugarpaste into a cone. Place this next to the arms.

3 Roll out a little white sugarpaste and cut out a triangle for the nappy. Stick it in place.

4 Divide 10g (1/3oz) flesh sugarpaste in half for the legs. Bend them into chunky "S" shapes and stick in position.

5 Roll 15g (1/2oz) flesh sugarpaste into a ball for the baby's head. Add two white disks for eyes and a tiny flesh ball for the nose.

6 Poke the end of a paintbrush into the head to create a mouth. Add two black dots for eyes and dab a little watery red food colour on the cheeks. Use the edge of a drinking straw to create eyebrows.

7 Stick the head in place and add two little flesh balls for ears. Poke the end of a paintbrush into each ear.

8 Make a tiny squiggle of brown sugarpaste for the baby's hair and stick onto his head.

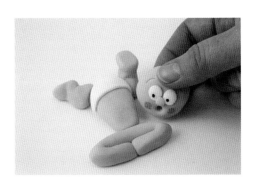

Faces and Expressions

There are many ways to create faces on your characters. Here are a few ideas to get you started. Probably the most important one to master though is a great big smile.

Basic Faces

1 Most simple faces begin as a sugarpaste ball or oval. You can either create the face off the cake then carefully stick it in place or in situ on the character.

2 Add two eyes. These can be as simple as two dots applied with a cocktail stick dipped in black food colour. Alternatively you could use a black food colour pen. Or stick two tiny white sugarpaste balls onto the face then add a food colour dot.

3 Stick three tiny sugarpaste balls onto the face with a little water for the ears and nose. To add a little detail to the ears poke a small hollow with the end of a paintbrush. This also presses the ears securely against the head.

4 Add a mouth. You could press a curved smile into the soft sugarpaste with a piping nozzle or paint a mouth onto the face using food colour.

5 A simple way to make hair is to dip a little sugarpaste in water then roll it in your fingers until it's sticky.

6 Place it onto the head and tease it into position with a cocktail stick.

Expressions and Emotions

Creating different expressions and emotions on simple sugarpaste faces is not as difficult as you might think. With a few dots, lines and the end of a paintbrush you'll be amazed at the myriad of expressions you can soon create. You can also draw on faces with a black food colour pen but allow the sugarpaste to harden first so you don't tear the surface.

Here are a few ideas to get you started.

Happy 1	**Happy 2**	**Sad**	**Doubtful**	**Surprised**

The easiest way to create a smile is to press a curved line using something like a piping nozzle. The hair on this character is created using a few wiggly strands of brown sugarpaste.	To create more of an open mouthed smile, press the piping nozzle into the icing and pull downwards slightly. If you want to add teeth, stick a tiny sliver of white sugarpaste inside the mouth. Use the edge of a drinking straw to create cheeks either side of the mouth.	Press a piping nozzle into the face the opposite way to the smile and you instantly create a very glum looking chap.	To make the eyes look more hooded, two small oval hollows were made with a bone tool (or you could use the end of a paintbrush) before sticking the eyeballs in place. The eyelids are a small flattened sugarpaste disk cut in half and stuck at an angle over each eye. The mouth was made using a piping nozzle.	Raised eyebrows (created with a drinking straw) and an open mouth (created with the end of a paintbrush) combine to create a very surprised expression.

Singing

It's surprisingly easy to make a little character appear to be singing their heart out. Poke the end of a paintbrush into the mouth area and gently pull it downwards to create a deep oval shape.

Screaming

Use a ball tool or the end of a wooden spoon to create an enormous hollow for the mouth. The creased up eyes are created using three small marks made with either a cocktail stick or the tip of a craft knife. The tooth is optional but works well if you are making a baby or toddler.

Whistling

To make your models whistle, stick a small ball of sugarpaste onto the mouth area and poke a small hole in the centre with a cocktail stick. The girl's plaits are made of strings of black sugarpaste twisted together. Her eyebrows have been painted on with black food colour.

Puzzled

The eyes and mouth are black food colour dots. The ears and nose, tiny balls of flesh coloured sugarpaste. The eyebrows that add such a dramatic effect to this expression are made with the edge of a drinking straw.

Embarrassed

A light brush of edible red dusting powder or a dab of watered down red food colour on the cheeks will immediately make your character look embarrassed. The mouth is made with the end of a paintbrush and the eyes, two dots made with the tip of a cocktail stick dipped into black food colour. The eyebrows are two slanted black food colour lines.

Angry

If you can write the letter "S" you can paint a pair of angry eyebrows on your little character. The eyes are three little lines made with the tip of a craft knife or cocktail stick and the cheeks are a made with a little edible red dusting powder or you could use a little watered down red food colour. The hair is a strip of brown sugarpaste with lines pressed along it. You may find it easiest to stick the strip onto the head then use the back of your knife to press an off centre line for the parting. It is also best to stick the ears onto the head after the hair is in place.

Baby

You don't need a huge amount of artistic ability to create a cute baby face. The mouth was created with a piping nozzle, the cheeks and chin with the edge of a drinking straw. The eyes are just two black food colour dots and the eyelashes, little cuts made with the tip of a craft knife. (You could use a cocktail stick to make them if you prefer.) The ears are two little balls stuck on the side of the head with small hollows made with the end of a paintbrush and the hair is just a small string of sugarpaste piled on top of the head.

Facial Hair

To add beards, moustaches and even magnificent bushy eyebrows, roll out a little sugarpaste and cut out a triangle for a beard or tear drop shapes for eyebrows or a moustache. Press a few lines into the sugarpaste with the back of your knife and stick the components in place. The tiny mouth on the character here was made with the tip of a drinking straw.

Make Up

Sometimes you might want to add a bit of glamour to your characters. Make a hollow eye socket with a bone tool or the end of a paintbrush and dab a little blue food colour inside. Add a small ball of white for the eye. Using a fine paintbrush and a little black food colour, paint a "U" shaped pupil and a curved arched line for the eyebrow. Paint a line around the top of the eye socket and three tiny eyelashes. Add a tiny ball of sugarpaste for the nose.

The lips are painted with red food colour. The top lip is a painted "M" shape and the lower lip just a curved line. The hair is a strip of coloured sugarpaste. Press lines down the length and stick on top of the head. Press a parting just off centre using the back of your knife.

Sneaky

Press a straight line with the back of a knife to create the mouth. Press a short line at either end of the mouth. Add eyes, ears and nose. The eyebrows can be either painted or drawn on with food colour. One eyebrow resembles a back to front tick, the other is an arched line. The hair is a string of sugarpaste coiled up at one end.

Glasses

An easy way to create glasses on your characters is with a drinking straw. Press two circles with the end of the straw onto the face and a line at the side of each circle with a knife. Add ears, nose and hair and black food colour dots for the eyes and mouth.

Goofy

Press a piping nozzle at an angle to create an off centre smile. Press a drinking straw at one end of the mouth to create a cheek. Stick two white ovals on the face for the eyes and paint a black food colour "U" shape on either eye. For the eyelids, create a small flat flesh coloured disk and cut in half. Stick one eyelid at an angle over each eye. The hair is a sticky lump of sugarpaste dipped in water and teased into an irregular shape. Add two flesh coloured ball shapes for the ears and press a hollow into either ear with the end of a paintbrush. Finally place a sliver of white sugarpaste into the mouth using a soft paintbrush and gently push it into place.

Old Lady

Make two hollows for the eyes with a bone tool or the end of a paintbrush. Add two white disks for eyes. Paint pupils onto the eyes. Use a drinking straw to press two circles for the glasses and press a line either side of the head for the arms of the glasses. Using a star tool or the end of a paintbrush press a circular mouth. Make a grey sugarpaste semi-circle for the hair. Press lines into the grey with the back of a knife and stick over the head. Press a centre parting into the middle. Make a small grey semi-circle for her bun. Press lines into the bun and stick on top of her head. Add ears and a nose to finish.

Positioning Characters

It is always worth considering whether the cake itself can help you when it comes to positioning your characters on your cake. If you need to make a standing figure for example it may be that you can use the sides of the cake to help support the figure. Another form of secret support is spaghetti. Poke a short length of spaghetti into your character and it should help keep them upright as the sugarpaste hardens. However even though it is edible, it is best to always let the recipient know when any internal supports are being used.

Sitting on the cake

This is the easiest way to display a figure on your cake.

You will need

30g (1oz) light brown sugarpaste
30g (1oz) red sugarpaste
15g (1/2oz) flesh coloured sugarpaste
10g dark brown sugarpaste
2 tiny white sugarpaste dots
1 strand raw uncooked spaghetti
Black food colour

Equipment

Small sharp knife
Drinking straw
Small rolling pin
Paintbrush

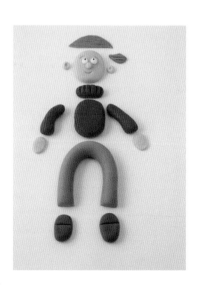

1 Make a thick 20g (2/3oz) brown sugarpaste string for the legs and bend into a "U" shape. Stick this onto the cake.

2 Make a small red 15g (1/2oz) oval shape for his body and stick this on top of the legs. Make a small red disk for the polo neck and stick on top of the body. Press lines around the neck with the back of a knife.

3 Poke a short length of spaghetti into the body leaving a little protruding from the neck. Make two 5g (1/8oz) red strings for the arms and stick against the body. Add two little flesh coloured ovals for his hands.

4 Create a 10g (1/3oz) flesh coloured oval for his head, Add two tiny white balls for his eyes and a flesh coloured ball for his nose. Use the edge of a drinking straw to make a mouth and eye brows.

5 Make a semi-circle of brown sugarpaste for his hair. Press lines into the hair with the back of a knife and stick over the top of the head. Make a tiny brown almond shape for the fringe. Press a few lines into it and stick onto his forehead. Paint two black dots on the eyes.

6 Make two tiny flesh coloured balls for his ears. Stick on to the head and poke the end of a paintbrush into each ear to create a little hollow.

7 Finally make two small dark brown ovals for his shoes. Press a line into the sole of each shoe and stick onto the ends of his legs.

Positioning Characters

Sitting on the Board

Another easy way to position your figure is to sit him on the board itself. The character can then lean against the side of the cake for support.

You will need

30g (1oz) blue sugarpaste
60g (2oz) brown sugarpaste
30g (1oz) flesh coloured sugarpaste
Tiny bits of white & black sugarpaste

Equipment

Paintbrush
Drinking straw
Small sharp knife
Small rolling pin
Piping nozzle

1 Make a 30g blue string for the legs and cross them over at the knees. Add a 30g (1oz) brown oval for the body and stick onto the legs.

2 Make two small brown sausage shapes for the arms. Bend them at the elbows and stick them in place. Add two small flesh coloured disks for hands.

3 Make a 15g (1/2oz) flesh coloured oval for the head. Poke the end of a piping nozzle into the face to create a mouth. Pull it downwards slightly to open the mouth a little. Stick two white ovals onto the face for his eyes. Stick a sliver of white inside the mouth for teeth.

4 Use a drinking straw to press two eyebrows. Stick two tiny black sugarpaste dots on the eyes. Roll out a small strip of brown sugarpaste for the hair. Press lines down the length with the back of a knife. Lay and stick the hair over the head and press a parting into the hair with the back of your knife.

5 Add two tiny flesh balls for ears and a third for a nose. Finally stick two brown ovals onto the ends of his trousers to create his shoes.

Sitting on the Edge

Legs dangling over the side of the cake is quite a fun way to display your characters.

You will need

20g (2/3oz) red sugarpaste
15g (1/2oz) yellow sugarpaste
60g (2oz) flesh coloured sugarpaste
Tiny bit of white and black sugarpaste
1 strand raw uncooked spaghetti
1 tbsp brown coloured royal icing or buttercream

Equipment

Paintbrush
Drinking straw
Small sharp knife
Small rolling pin
Piping nozzle (No 2 or 3)

1 Roll the red sugarpaste into a string for the trousers. Bend it into a "U" shape. Stick it onto the edge of the cake. Make a yellow sugarpaste torso and stick on top of the legs.

2 Make a small flesh oval for the neck and stick on top of the body. Poke a section of spaghetti through the neck and body and into the cake below. Make a 10g (1/3oz) flesh ball for the head. Press a piping nozzle into the head and pull it downwards a little to create the mouth.

3 Stick two white disks on the face for her eyes and a sliver of white into her mouth to create teeth. Add pupils to the eyes.

4 Using a drinking straw, press curved cheeks either side of the mouth. Create eyelashes with the tip of your knife. Stick the head into place on the body.

5 Make two 5g (1/8oz) thin flesh strings for her arms and two small brown "L" shaped boots and stick onto the ends of the legs and against the cake.

6 The model's wonderful curls were achieved by piping a little brown coloured royal icing or buttercream in swirls all over her head.

Positioning Characters

Bursting out of the cake

Ta Dah! Not only is this a fun way to present a character on your cake, you don't have to bother with legs and feet!

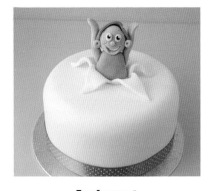

Bursting out of the side of the cake

This is best done after the sugarpaste covering the cake has set overnight. This makes the weight of the model less likely to tear the icing. Keep the body and head as slim as possible and stick securely against the cake.

You will need

30g (1oz) pink sugarpaste
30g (1oz) flesh coloured sugarpaste
Tiny bit of black sugarpaste
5g (1/8oz) brown sugarpaste
45g (1 1/2oz) white sugarpaste

Equipment

Paintbrush
Piping nozzle
Drinking straw
Small sharp knife
Small rolling pin

You will need

20g (2/3oz) green sugarpaste
15g (1/2oz) flesh coloured sugarpaste
5g (1/8oz) black sugarpaste
45g (1 1/2oz) white sugarpaste
Black food colour
Water
1 strand raw uncooked spaghetti

Equipment

Paintbrush
Piping nozzle
Drinking straw
Small sharp knife
Small rolling pin

1 Make a pink cone shape for the body and stick in the centre of the cake. Poke a little spaghetti inside the body for extra support if you wish.

2 Make a 15g (1/2oz) flesh coloured ball shape for the head. Press a piping nozzle into the lower part of the face and pull it downwards to open the mouth. Make two tiny white ovals for the eyes and stick in place. Stick a sliver of white inside the mouth for teeth.

3 Use a drinking straw to make cheeks and eyebrows. Add tiny dots of black and white sugarpaste to the eyes to create the pupils. Slot the head into position on the body. Roll out a little brown sugarpaste for the hair. Cut out a rectangle and press lines down its length with the back of your knife. Stick the hair onto the head and press a parting on one side.

4 Make two 5g (1/8oz) flesh sugarpaste arms and stick against the body. Tweak the hands so they point outwards. Add ears and a nose.

5 Roll out about 45g (1 1/2oz) white sugarpaste and cut out five or six triangles. Stick these around the character.

1 Begin by sticking a 10g (1/3oz) green oval for the body onto the cake. Don't make it too thick or it will simply fall off.

2 Make a 10g (1/3 oz) flesh coloured disk for the head. Add two tiny white ovals for the eyes. Use a piping nozzle to make the mouth and the edge of a drinking straw to create the cheeks, chin and eyebrows.

3 Paint black food colour pupils on the eyes and add a nose and two ears.

4 Poke the end of a paintbrush into each ear to create a small hollow. Stick the head onto the body and against the cake. You could poke a little spaghetti through the top of the head into the cake if you wish.

5 Dip a little black sugarpaste in water and rough it up in your fingers. Stick a little bit onto the head to form his hair.

6 Make two 5g (1/8oz) green sausage shapes for the arms and two flat disks for the hands. Make a little cut in each hand to create a thumb. Stick the arms and hands against the cake.

7 Roll out the white sugarpaste and cut out about six small white triangles and stick these around your character.

Positioning Characters

Standing

Here's an easy way to create a standing character. Use the side of the cake for support. Let's face it, it doesn't get more difficult than being asked to create a ballerina on pointe!

You will need

30g (1oz) pink sugarpaste
30g (1oz) flesh coloured sugarpaste
Tiny bit of black sugarpaste
5g (1/8oz) brown sugarpaste
45g (1 1/2oz) white sugarpaste

Equipment

Paintbrush
Piping nozzle
Drinking straw
Small sharp knife
Small rolling pin

1 Use about 10g (1/3oz) flesh coloured sugarpaste for the legs. Roll it into two strings and stick them onto the side of the cake. Make two tiny pink feet and place into position.

2 Add a 5g (1/8oz) pink oval for her torso and poke a short length of spaghetti through the body and into the cake for added support. To make the frilly skirt, roll out 10g (1/3oz) pink sugarpaste and cut out a small rectangle. Press or roll the end of a paintbrush repeatedly along its length. It should create a frilly effect. Stick the skirt in place.

3 Make a 5g (1/8oz) head and stick on to the body. Make the eyes, eyebrows and mouth with the edge of a drinking straw. Add two thin sugarpaste strings for the arms and a tiny nose.

4 Make a flat black semi-circle for the hair. Press a few lines into it with the back of the knife and stick it over the head. Press a centre parting in the middle with the back of a knife.

5 Stick a small pink disk on top of the head and top with a little black ball for her bun. Ears: stick two flesh coloured balls on the side of her head and poke the end of a paintbrush into either ear.

Bride and Groom

This is the only design in the book that uses a special cutter. It's called a blossom plunge cutter which cuts out tiny little flowers quickly and easily. These little cutters are widely available from cake decorating stockists but you could always pipe flowers or just use dots of sugarpaste if you prefer.

Groom

You will need

100g (3 1/2oz) black sugarpaste
10g (1/3oz) white sugarpaste
5g (1/8oz) pink sugarpaste
30g (1oz) flesh coloured sugarpaste
10g (1/3oz) brown sugarpaste
Tiny dot of yellow sugarpaste
1 strand raw uncooked spaghetti
Water for sticking
Icing sugar

Equipment

Paintbrushes (fine & medium)
Small sharp knife
Small rolling pin
Piping nozzle (any design)
Drinking straw
Blossom plunge cutter (optional)

1 Begin with the legs. Roll 30g (1oz) black sugarpaste into a string about 15cm (6in) long and bend into a horseshoe shape.

2 Mould 30g (1oz) black sugarpaste into a cone for his body and stick on top of the legs. Poke a little spaghetti into the body for extra support if you wish.

3 Roll out a little white sugarpaste and cut out a small triangle for his shirt. Stick this onto his chest. Stick a tiny pink string on top of the white for his tie and press a line across it with the back of your knife.

4 Cut out a tiny white rectangle for the shirt collar. Make a partial cut across the centre and stick the collar over the tie. The cut should splay apart around the tie.

5 To make the suit lapels, cut out a long thin strip of black sugarpaste. Make a little diagonal cut at each end. Lay and stick this around the white triangle, collar and neck.

6 Make a 15g (1/2oz) flesh coloured ball for the head. Press a mouth with a piping nozzle and cheeks with the edge of a drinking straw. Add eyes and a nose.

7 Cut out a semi-circle of brown sugarpaste for his hair. Press lines into it with the back of your knife and stick over the head. Make a tiny almond shape for his fringe. Press lines into that too and stick onto his forehead.

8 Cut out a small black disk for the brim of his hat. Shape about 5g (1/8oz) black sugarpaste into a cylindrical shape for the top of the hat. Stick the two together on top of his head.

9 Roll about 15g (1/2oz) black sugarpaste into a string for the arms. Cut it in half and stick one arm either side of the body.

10 Make two small flesh ovals for the hands and stick as though holding the hat brim.

11 Add two tiny flesh ball shapes for the ears and stick onto the head. Roll out a little pink and cut out a flower with the plunge cutter. Stick the flower onto his lapel. Add a tiny yellow sugarpaste dot in the centre.

12 Make two 5g (1/8oz) black ovals for his feet and stick on the end of the legs.

Bride and Groom

Bride

You will need

90g (3oz) white sugarpaste
30g (1oz) flesh coloured sugarpaste
5g (1/8oz) pink sugarpaste
15g (1/2oz) yellow sugarpaste
1 strand spaghetti
Black food colour
Water for sticking
Icing sugar

Equipment

Paintbrushes fine & medium
Small sharp knife
Blossom plunge cutter (optional)
Drinking straw

1 Mould 45g (1 1/2oz) white sugarpaste into a thick semi-circle shape for the bride's skirt.

2 Make a 10g (1/3oz) white oval for her body and stick this on top of the skirt. Poke a little spaghetti down the centre for support if you wish.

3 Add a small disk of flesh coloured sugarpaste for her neck.

4 Roll about 5g (1/8oz) flesh sugarpaste into a string for her arms. Bend it into a "U" shape and stick onto her front.

5 Roll out a little pink sugarpaste. Cut out three plunge cutter blossoms and stick them on her arms to form a bouquet.

6 Make a 10g (1/3oz) flesh sugarpaste ball for her head. Add two tiny white eyes and create a smile with the edge of a drinking straw. Press eyelashes with the tip of a knife and paint pupils onto the eyes. Use a tiny flesh dot for her nose.

7 Thinly roll out about 15g (1/2oz) yellow sugarpaste. Cut out a long rectangle for her hair. Press lines into it with the back of your knife and drape over the head. Add a tiny almond shaped fringe.

8 To make the veil, thinly roll out 20g (2/3oz) white sugarpaste. Cut out a tapering rectangle and stick onto the back of her head.

9 Stick a line of pink blossoms with yellow centres on top of her head.

10 Stick a line of white plunge cutter blossoms along the hem of her dress and add two tiny white ovals for her feet.

Teddy Bears

Everyone loves teddy bears so there had to be a short section on them. Obviously you can make your bears in whatever colour you want but if you want to go for the traditional golden brown colour, you can buy ready coloured sugarpaste in a shade called rather aptly "Teddy bear Brown" or colour white sugarpaste using a food colour paste in a shade called "Autumn Leaf". Once you can make a bear there are all sorts of ways you can adapt him. Pop an icing Santa hat on his head for instance and immediately he becomes a Seasonal Christmas Bear !

Bear

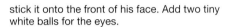

stick it onto the front of his face. Add two tiny white balls for the eyes.

6 Stick two brown balls on the top of his head for his ears and poke a small hollow into each ear with the end of a paintbrush.

7 Divide 5g (1/8oz) brown sugarpaste in half and make two tiny sausage shapes for his arms. Stick one either side of the body. Press a couple of lines into the end of each paw with the tip of your knife.

8 Either paint or stick a black sugarpaste oval onto the muzzle for his nose, paint two black food colour dots onto the eyes and a "W" or a curved smile under the nose for his mouth.

1 Roll about 30g (1oz) golden brown sugarpaste into a cone. The top must be flattish so the head doesn't fall off. Make a 10g (1/3oz) ball for the head and stick this on top of the body.

2 Stick a small, flat white sugarpaste oval onto his tummy.

3 Roll about 10g (1/3oz) sugarpaste into a sausage for the legs. Cut it in half and bend each leg into an "L" shape.

4 Stick the legs around the body and poke four small hollows into the base of each foot with the end of a paintbrush to create the paw.

You will need

60g (2oz) golden brown coloured sugarpaste
10g (1/3oz) white sugarpaste
Tiny bit of black sugarpaste (optional)
Black food colour paste
Icing sugar
Water for sticking

Equipment

Paintbrushes (fine & medium)
Small sharp knife

Teddy Bears

This little character would be ideal for a Christening cake or a first birthday. If it's for a little boy you may want to change the colour scheme and not include the bow though!

Baby Bear

You will need

45g (1 1/2oz) golden brown sugarpaste
5g (1/8 oz) white sugarpaste
45g (1 1/2oz) pink sugarpaste
15g (1/2oz) dark brown sugarpaste
Tiny bit of black sugarpaste
Black food colour
Icing sugar
Water for sticking sugarpaste

Equipment

Paintbrushes (fine & medium)
Craft knife or similar
Small sharp knife
Cocktail Stick
Small rolling pin

1 Make a 30g (1oz) golden brown cone for the bear's body and stick a 10g (1/3oz) oval for the head on top.

2 Add a white oval muzzle and two flattened white balls for eyes. Make two tiny cuts either side of the eyes with the tip of a knife for eyelashes. Paint two black dots on the eyes.

3 Stick two tiny brown balls on top of the head for the ears and press a hollow into each one with the end of a paintbrush.

4 Make two tiny pink triangles and a tiny ball for the bow. Press a couple of lines into each triangle and stick them onto the head. Stick the ball in the centre.

5 Stick a tiny black oval nose onto the muzzle.

6 To make the dummy, make a tiny pink disk and stick a tiny pink ball in the centre. Poke a hole into the ball with the tip of a cocktail stick.

7 Make a smaller teddy head in a darker or contrasting colour for the toy and stick against the body.

8 Thinly roll out about 30g (1oz) pink sugarpaste and cut out a rectangle 18cm x 5cm (7in x 2in). Press diagonal lines with the back of your knife across the rectangle to create a criss cross pattern.

9 Wrap and stick the blanket around the teddy.

10 Make a small golden brown sausage shape for the paw and stick beneath the toy teddy and onto the edge of the blanket as though holding it. Press a couple of lines into the end of the paw.

Teddy Bears

The teddy bears' picnic has become quite a classic cake design but in a section on teddy bears it deserves another outing. Of course your picnic doesn't have to be confined to just teddy bears, you could invite any of the other characters in the book along too! If you want to give your bears food to hold, make the food first.

Teddy Bears' Picnic

You will need

Three assembled bears
15cm (6in) covered cake
30g (1oz) yellow sugarpaste
150g (5oz) white sugarpaste
5g (1/8oz) red sugarpaste

Equipment

Small rolling pin
Small sharp knife
Paintbrush
Cocktail stick

1. Make a bear following the instructions for making a basic bear apart from the instruction for putting an oval of white on his tummy. Instead, make a little napkin by rolling out a little yellow sugarpaste. Cut out a square and stick it on to his front. Do this before you put the head on so it looks as though it's tucked under his chin.

2. To make the picnic, first make some plates. Roll out a little yellow sugarpaste and cut out two or three flat disks using a small circle cutter or lid.

Sandwiches

To make a jam sandwich, thinly roll out two small strips of white sugarpaste and one red. Stick all three layers together with the red in the middle. Cut a long rectangle and divide into squares then triangles. Stack the sandwiches onto a plate. Keep a couple to one side for the bears to hold. To make it look as though it's been eaten, use a drinking straw to take a "bite" out of a sandwich.

Biscuits

Make some tiny little flattened brown disks and poke a few holes in the top with a cocktail stick.

Buns

Make a few small round brown disks and top with a smaller white disk and a tiny red sugarpaste ball.

Rug

Thinly roll out about 90g (3oz) white sugarpaste and cut out a square. Lay on the cake and paint blue food colour lines across the rug. They don't have to be perfectly straight. Arrange and stick the bears and food in place.

Little Animals - Dog With Ball

If your dog likes to get filthy when he's out you could daub a little chocolate buttercream on your model to create a muddy look.

tennis racquet shape then roll the thick part towards the "handle". Stick against the body with the foot pointing forwards.

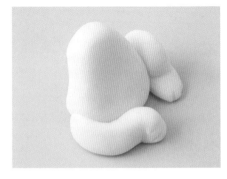

3 The front legs are little sausage shapes. Press a couple of lines into the front of each paw with the back of your knife.

4 Stick a red disk on top of the body to create a collar. Stick a tiny brown ball immediately below it for the dog tag.

5 Use 10g (1/3oz) white sugarpaste to make the head shape. Cut across the muzzle to create a mouth. Splay the mouth open slightly. Make a tiny pink tongue and pop it inside.

6 Make a little white sugarpaste string for the tail and stick it on his rear. Make two eyes out of tiny white disks and two black sugarpaste dots.

7 Make a tiny black oval for his nose and two black triangles for ears and stick them all in place.

8 To make a mat, thinly roll out about 15g (1/2oz) green sugarpaste and cut out a rectangle. Press lines across the mat with the back of your knife and cut a fringe along the two ends.

You will need

45g (1 1/2oz) white sugarpaste
5g (1/8oz) black sugarpaste
Tiny bits of red, brown and pink sugarpastes
15g (1/2oz) green sugarpaste
5g (1/8oz) blue sugarpaste
Water for sticking
Icing sugar

Equipment

Small sharp knife
Small rolling pin
Paintbrush

1 Make a 15g (1/2oz) cone shape for the dog's body and stand it upright.

2 For the legs you will need 10g (1/3oz) white sugarpaste. Make a sausage shape for the back left leg then bend it into an "S" shape and stick around the body. To make the back right leg, make a

Little Animals - Puppy in Handbag

Now although I do not see dogs as a fashion accessory, the combination of a dog and a handbag does make an endearing cake accessory.

3 To make the dog's body, use about 5g (1/8oz) brown sugarpaste. Create a shape a bit like a tangerine segment.

4 Scratch the top of the dog's back with a Dresden tool or cocktail stick to give a hairy effect and slot the body into the handbag.

5 Roll about 5g (1/8oz) brown sugarpaste into an oval for the dog's face. Scratch it with the Dresden tool and poke a hole for the mouth with the end of a paintbrush. Stick the head onto the dog's body in the handbag.

6 Stick three tiny black sugarpaste dots onto the face for the eyes and nose. Poke a tiny bit of pink into the mouth to create a tongue.

7 Make two tiny brown strips for the eyebrows. Scratch them with the Dresden tool and stick an eyebrow at an angle over each eye. Stick a tiny white sugarpaste dot on each eye for highlights.

You will need

45g (1 1/2oz) pink sugarpaste
20g (2/3oz) golden brown sugarpaste
3 tiny black sugarpaste dots & two white
Water for sticking
Icing sugar

Equipment

Small sharp knife
Dresden tool or cocktail stick
Paintbrush

1 To make the handbag, mould 30g (1oz) pink sugarpaste into a thick semi-circle. Press a criss cross pattern into the sides with the back of a knife.

2 Slice the bag from the top to about halfway down and gently splay the two sides apart to create an opening.

8 Make two little brown triangles for the ears and a short stubby tail. Scratch all three and stick them in place.

9 Make a short pink string for the handbag handle and stick onto the side of the bag. Make two tiny brown dots and stick them onto the ends of the handle. Poke the end of a paintbrush into both dots.

Little Animals - Cat

Feel free to personalise the colours of the cat's coat to resemble the favourite moggy in your life!

2 Make the paws out of a thick white disk. Cut it into quarters and stick two paws at the front and the other two at the side. Press two lines into each paw with the back of your knife.

3 Make a 20g (2/3oz) brown oval for the head. Then pinch the sides and tweak into points and stick on top of the body.

4 To make the mouth, squash a tiny ball of pink onto a slightly larger squashed ball of white and stick onto the bottom of the face.

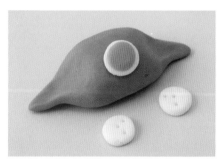

5 Make two tiny flat white disks for the muzzle and stick over the mouth leaving the bottom of the mouth showing. Poke three tiny holes in each side of the muzzle with a cocktail stick.

6 Stick two small white ovals above the muzzle for the eyes. Paint pupils on the eyes with black food colour.

7 To make the eyelids, make a little flat brown disk and slice in half. Stick one half over each eye at an angle.

8 For the ears, make a pink triangle and stick onto a slightly larger brown one. Stick the ears on top of the head.

9 To finish, make a brown string for the tail and stick a white point on the tip. Paint a few black food colour stripes on the front and head of the cat.

You will need

60g (2oz) golden brown coloured sugarpaste
10g (1/3oz) white sugarpaste
5g (1/8oz) pink sugarpaste
Black food colour paste
Water for sticking
Icing sugar

Equipment

Small sharp knife
Paintbrush
Small rolling pin
Cocktail stick

1 Create the body using 30g (1oz) brown sugarpaste. Press a line into the front of the body using the back of your knife.

Little Animals - Horse

Vary the colouring and markings of your icing horse to make it resemble the recipient's favourite pony. You could make him a few orange sugarpaste carrots too.

You will need

130g (4 1/2oz) brown sugarpaste
15g (1/2oz) black sugarpaste
5g (1/8oz) white sugarpaste
Water for sticking
Icing sugar

Equipment

Paintbrush
Piping nozzle
Small rolling pin
Small sharp knife
Cocktail Stick

1 To make the body of the horse, shape 60g (2oz) brown sugarpaste into a carrot shape and lay on its side.

2 Make a 5g (1/8oz) brown oval shape for the neck and stick this on top of the thinnest part of the cone.

3 Divide 15g (1/2oz) brown sugarpaste in half and roll into two small sausage shapes for the front legs. Bend them almost in half and stick one either side of the neck.

4 To make the back leg, roll 15g (1/2oz) brown sugarpaste into a sausage then squash one end to create a sort of tennis racquet shape. Roll the rounded end towards the straight section to create the leg shape and stick at the rear of the horse.

5 Use 30g (1oz) brown sugarpaste for the head. Roll it into a chunky sausage shape then gently squeeze the middle. Use the edge of a piping nozzle to create a mouth and poke two nostrils with the end of a paint brush.

6 Stick two white ovals onto the face for his eyes. Add two tiny black sugarpaste pupils and two tiny white sugarpaste dots as highlights. Press three eyelashes either side of each eye with the tip of a knife or a cocktail stick.

7 Make two tiny brown carrot shapes for the ears. Press the end of a paintbrush flat on each ear to give them a bit of shape.

8 Using the rest of the black sugarpaste make the mane and tail. Create a sort of flat carrot shape for the tail and make three long partial cuts down its length. Stick onto the rear of the horse.

9 Make a tiny rectangle for the fringe and a larger one for the mane. Cut a fringe into both pieces and stick them on to the head.

Little Animals - Rabbit

A simple model that should make any rabbit owner smile any time of the year. Surround him with chocolate eggs in Spring and he instantly becomes the Easter bunny.

You will need

60g (2oz) grey sugarpaste
5g (1/8oz) white sugarpaste
Tiny bits of black and pink sugarpaste
Water for sticking
Icing sugar

Equipment

Small sharp knife
Paintbrush
Bone tool (optional)

1 Use 30g (1oz) grey sugarpaste to make the body.

2 Use 5g (1/8oz) grey sugarpaste to make all the legs. Make two tiny strings for the front legs. Use the rest to create two shapes that resemble the letter "P"

for the back legs. Stick all the legs in place and press a couple of lines with the back of your knife into the front of each leg to create paws.

3 Make a 10g grey oval for the head. Create two oval eye sockets with either a bone tool or the end of a paintbrush.

4 Stick two white rectangles for the teeth onto the face. Make and stick two tiny white ovals in to the eye sockets. Make a tiny white ball for a tail.

5 Stick two black eyeballs onto the white.

6 Make two flat white disks for the rabbit's muzzle and stick in place. The teeth should be visible below the bottom of the muzzle.

7 Press three lines into either side of the muzzle with the back of a knife and add a tiny pink ball for the nose.

8 Divide 5g (1/8oz) grey sugarpaste in half and make two small carrot shapes for the ears. Press the end of a level paintbrush into each ear to create a hollow line then stick the ears upright on the head.

Little Animals - Elephant

Although I am not entirely sure whether elephants are afraid of mice, it does make for an amusing cake decoration !

You will need

100g (3 1/2oz) grey sugarpaste
Tiny bits of black, white and pink sugarpaste
Black food colour paste
Water for sticking
Icing sugar

Equipment

Knife
Paintbrush
Drinking straw

1 Divide 20g (2/3oz) grey sugarpaste into three and make three thick disks for the legs. Arrange and stick next to each other on the cake leaving a space where the fourth leg should be.

2 Make a 30g (1oz) grey ball for the body and stick on top of the legs.

3 Create a cone shape for the fourth leg using 5g (1/8oz) grey sugarpaste and stick this onto the front of the body. Press toes into the legs using a drinking straw.

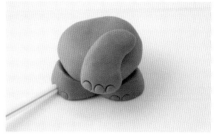

4 Use 30g (1oz) grey to create the head. Stick it onto the body so that the trunk rests on the ground. Press a couple lines across the trunk with the back of your knife and press two nostrils using the end of a paintbrush.

5 To make the mouth, poke the end of a paintbrush into the side of the elephant's face and pull downwards.

6 Roll 5g (1/8oz) grey into a thick disk and cut in half for the ears then stick them in place on the head. Make a tiny string for the tail and stick in place.

7 Stick two white sugarpaste ovals onto the front of the face for the eyes and stick two black sugarpaste disks on top. Add two tiny white sugarpaste dots as highlights.

8 Paint two curved black lines with food colour for the eyebrows.

9 To make the mouse, make a tiny grey oval. Add two tiny grey balls for the ears and two black dots for the eyes Make a tiny pink dot for the nose and a pink string for the tail.

Little Animals - Piggy Back

An easy way to create a nice muddy patch for your pigs to play in is to stand them in a blob of chocolate buttercream.

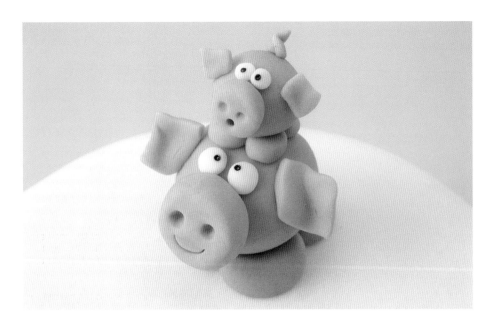

You will need

90g (3oz) pink sugarpaste
5g (1/8oz) white sugarpaste
Black food colour paste
Water for sticking
Icing sugar

Equipment

Small sharp knife
Drinking straw
Paintbrush

1 To make the big pig, divide 10g (1/3oz) pink sugarpaste into quarters and make four thick disks for the legs. Stick them side by side in a square formation.

2 Make a 25g (1oz) pink ball shape for the body and stick it on top of the legs.

3 Make a 5g (1/8oz) thick disk for the snout and stick it onto the front of the pig. Poke the edge of a drinking straw into the snout to make a mouth and use the end of a paintbrush to create nostrils.

4 Stick two tiny white sugarpaste balls onto the front of the face for the eyes and add two black food colour dots.

5 Thinly roll out about 5g (1/8oz) pink sugarpaste and cut out two small squares for the ears. Press and stick them against the side of the head.

6 Use some of the leftover pink to make a thin string for the tail.

7 To make the little pig, repeat these instructions but make him much smaller and stand him on top of the larger one.

Little Animals - Cheeky Monkey

Most families have a "cheeky monkey" somewhere amongst their ranks so there's quite a good chance this little chap will be going to a lot of parties !

2 Make a 20g (2/3oz) ball for the head and stick on top of the body. Stick two light brown disks onto the face for his eyes and an oval for the muzzle.

3 Press a piping nozzle into the muzzle to create a smile.

4 Stick two tiny dark brown sugarpaste dots on the eyes and one as a nose. Stick two teeny weeny white sugarpaste dots on the eyes as highlights.

5 Make a banana shape with the yellow sugarpaste. Divide 5g (1/8oz) dark brown sugarpaste in half and make two long strings for the arms. Stick onto the body and place the banana in one of the hands.

6 To make the ears, stick two small brown ball shapes on the side of the head and poke the end of a paintbrush into each one.

You will need

60g (2oz) dark brown sugarpaste
5g (1/8oz) light brown sugarpaste
Tiny bit of yellow and white sugarpaste
Water for sticking
Icing sugar

Equipment

Small sharp knife
Paintbrush
Piping nozzle

1 Roll 20g (2/3oz) dark brown sugarpaste into a ball for the body. Divide 5g (1/8oz) dark brown in half and create two "L" shapes for the legs. Stick the legs around the body.

Cake Decorating Tools

You do not need a vast amount of equipment to make the cake characters in this book. Although there are three specialist cake decorating items shown here, they are not essential as a wooden spoon, paintbrush and cocktail stick will work just as well.

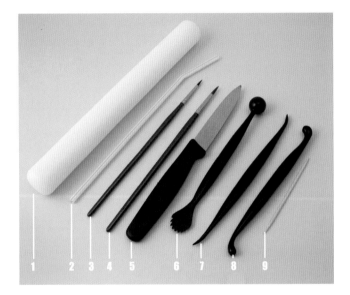

1 Small rolling pin.
This is useful as it means you don't have to wrestle with a huge rolling pin to roll a tiny bit of sugarpaste.
Don't have one?
Lie a paintbrush on its side and use that instead.

2 Drinking Straw
Cheap, cheerful and disposable. This is useful for making little smiles, cheeks, and eyebrows on your characters.

3 & 4 Paintbrushes
You will need a soft one for sticking your models together and a fine one for painting fine lines and faces.

5 Small sharp knife
A non serrated knife (one with a clean straight edge) can be used for all sorts as well as cutting. You can use it to press lines into soft sugarpaste and use the pointed tip to create eyelashes on your characters.

6 Ball tool
This is useful for creating shouty mouths on characters and large hollows but if you don't have one, use the end of a wooden spoon instead.

7 Dresden tool
This is useful for making scratchy fur effects and small lines but if you don't have one, a cocktail stick will usually work just as well.

8 Bone tool
Great for creating eye sockets and other small hollows on your models. If you don't have one, use the rounded end of a small paintbrush instead.

9 Cocktail Stick
Probably the cheapest yet the most versatile bit of kit shown here! Used for making fur effects, making frills, poking dots on cookies, creating mouths and eyes on teddies. The list goes on and on.